Made in the USA
Monee, IL
26 March 2022

93586121R00063